Lean and Green Cookbook: Quick and Easy to Follow Recipes to Rapid Weight Loss. Change Your Mindset and Start Living a Healthy Life.

Simona Mendoza

Table of Contents

Breakfast

Crunchy Quinoa Meal

Preparation Time: 5 minutes

Cooking Time: 25 minutes

Servings: 2

Ingredients:

- 3 cups coconut milk
- 1 cup rinsed quinoa
- 1/8 tsp. ground cinnamon
- 1 cup raspberry
- 1/2 cup chopped coconuts

Directions:

1. In a saucepan, pour milk and bring to a boil over moderate heat.
2. Add the quinoa to the milk and then bring it to a boil once more.
3. You then let it simmer for at least 15 minutes on medium heat until the milk is reduced.
4. Stir in the cinnamon then mix properly.
5. Cover it then cook for 8 minutes until the milk is completely absorbed.
6. Add the raspberry and cook the meal for 30 seconds.
7. Serve and enjoy.

Nutrition:

Calories: 271 kcal

Fat: 3.7g

Carbs: 54g

Proteins: 6.5g

Coconut Pancakes

Preparation Time: 5 minutes

Cooking Time: 15 minutes

Servings: 4

Ingredients:

- 1 cup coconut flour
- 2 tbsps. arrowroot powder
- 1 tsp. baking powder
- 1 cup coconut milk
- 3 tbsps. coconut oil

Directions:

1. In a medium container, mix in all the dry ingredients.
2. Add the coconut milk and 2 tbsps. of the coconut oil then mix properly.
3. In a skillet, melt 1 tsp. of coconut oil.
4. Pour a ladle of the batter into the skillet then swirl the pan to spread the batter evenly into a smooth pancake.
5. Cook it for like 3 minutes on medium heat until it becomes firm.
6. Turn the pancake to the other side then cook it for another 2 minutes until it turns golden brown.
7. Cook the remaining pancakes in the same process.
8. Serve.

Nutrition:

Calories: 377 kcal

Fat: 14.9g

Carbs: 60.7g

Protein: 6.4g

Quinoa Porridge

Preparation Time: 5 minutes

Cooking Time: 25 minutes

Servings: 2

Ingredients:

- 2 cups coconut milk
- 1 cup rinsed quinoa
- 1/8 tsp. ground cinnamon
- 1 cup fresh blueberries

Directions:

1. In a saucepan, boil the coconut milk over high heat.
2. Add the quinoa to the milk then bring the mixture to a boil.
3. You then let it simmer for 15 minutes on medium heat until the milk is reducing.
4. Add the cinnamon then mix it properly in the saucepan.
5. Cover the saucepan and cook for at least 8 minutes until milk is completely absorbed.
6. Add in the blueberries then cook for 30 more seconds.
7. Serve.

Nutrition:

Calories: 271 kcal

Fat: 3.7g

Carbs: 54g

Protein:6.5g

Amaranth Porridge

Preparation Time: 5 minutes

Cooking Time: 30 minutes

Servings: 2.

Ingredients:

- 2 cups coconut milk
- 2 cups alkaline water
- 1 cup amaranth
- 2 tbsps. coconut oil
- 1 tbsp. ground cinnamon

Directions:

1. In a saucepan, mix in the milk with water then boil the mixture.
2. You stir in the amaranth then reduce the heat to medium.
3. Cook on the medium heat then simmer for at least 30 minutes as you stir it occasionally.
4. Turn off the heat.
5. Add in cinnamon and coconut oil then stir.
6. Serve.

Nutrition:

Calories: 434 kcal

Fat: 35g

Carbs: 27g

Protein: 6.7g

Banana Barley Porridge

Preparation Time: 15 minutes

Cooking Time: 5 minutes

Servings: 2

Ingredients:

- 1 cup divided unsweetened coconut milk
- 1 small peeled and sliced banana
- 1/2 cup barley
- 3 drops liquid stevia
- 1/4 cup chopped coconuts

Directions:

1. In a bowl, properly mix barley with half of the coconut milk and stevia.
2. Cover the mixing bowl then refrigerate for about 6 hours.
3. In a saucepan, mix the barley mixture with coconut milk.
4. Cook for about 5 minutes on moderate heat.
5. Then top it with the chopped coconuts and the banana slices.
6. Serve.

Nutrition:

Calories: 159kcal

Fat: 8.4g

Carbs: 19.8g

Proteins: 4.6g

Zucchini Muffins

Preparation Time: 10 minutes

Cooking Time: 25 minutes

Servings: 16

Ingredients:

- 1 tbsp. ground flaxseed
- 3 tbsps. alkaline water
- 1/4 cup walnut butter
- 3 medium over-ripe bananas
- 2 small grated zucchinis
- 1/2 cup coconut milk
- 1 tsp. vanilla extract
- 2 cups coconut flour
- 1 tbsp. baking powder
- 1 tsp. cinnamon
- 1/4 tsp. sea salt

Directions:

1. Tune the temperature of your oven to 375°F.
2. Grease the muffin tray with the cooking spray.
3. In a bowl, mix the flaxseed with water.
4. In a glass bowl, mash the bananas then stir in the remaining ingredients.
5. Properly mix and then divide the mixture into the muffin tray.

6. Bake it for 25 minutes.

7. Serve.

Nutrition:

Calories: 127 kcal

Fat: 6.6g

Carbs: 13g

Protein: 0.7g

Millet Porridge

Preparation Time: 10 minutes

Cooking Time: 20 minutes

Servings: 2

Ingredients:

- Sea salt
- 1 tbsp. finely chopped coconuts
- 1/2 cup unsweetened coconut milk
- 1/2 cup rinsed and drained millet
- 1-1/2 cups alkaline water
- 3 drops liquid stevia

Directions:

1. Sauté the millet in a non-stick skillet for about 3 minutes.
2. Add salt and water then stir.
3. Let the meal boil then reduce the amount of heat.
4. Cook for 15 minutes then add the remaining ingredients. Stir.
5. Cook the meal for 4 extra minutes.
6. Serve the meal with toping of the chopped nuts.

Nutrition:

Calories: 219 kcal

Fat: 4.5g

Carbs: 38.2g

Protein: 6.4g

Lunch

Tropical Greens Smoothie

Preparation Time: 5 Minutes

Cooking Time: 0 Minutes

Servings: 1

Ingredients:

- One banana
- 1/2 large navel orange, peeled and segmented
- 1/2 cup frozen mango chunks
- 1 cup frozen spinach
- One celery stalk, broken into pieces
- One tablespoon cashew butter or almond butter
- 1/2 tablespoon spiraling
- 1/2 tablespoon ground flaxseed
- 1/2 cup unsweetened nondairy milk
- Water, for thinning (optional)

Directions:

1. In a high-speed blender or food processor, combine the bananas, orange, mango, spinach, celery, cashew butter, spiraling (if using), flaxseed, and milk.
2. Blend until creamy, adding more milk or water to thin the smoothie if too thick. Serve immediately—it is best served fresh.

Nutrition:

Calories: 391

Fat: 12g

Protein: 13g

Carbohydrates: 68g

Fiber: 13g

Vitamin C Smoothie Cubes

Preparation Time: 5 Minutes

Cooking Time: 8 Hours to chill

Servings: 1

Ingredients:

- 1/8 large papaya
- 1/8 mango
- 1/4 cups chopped pineapple, fresh or frozen
- 1/8 cup raw cauliflower florets, fresh or frozen
- 1/4 large navel oranges, peeled and halved
- 1/4 large orange bell pepper stemmed, seeded, and coarsely chopped

Directions:

1. Halve the papaya and mango, remove the pits, and scoop their soft flesh into a high-speed blender.
2. Add the pineapple, cauliflower, oranges, and bell pepper. Blend until smooth.
3. Evenly divide the puree between 2 (16-compartment) ice cube trays and place them on a level surface in your freezer. Freeze for at least 8 hours.
4. The cubes can be left in the ice cube trays until use or transferred to a freezer bag. The frozen cubes are good for about three weeks in a standard freezer or up to 6 months in a chest freezer.

Nutrition:

Calories: 96

Fat: <1g

Protein: 2g

Carbohydrates: 24g

Fiber: 4g

Overnight Chocolate Chia Pudding

Preparation Time: 2 Minutes

Cooking Time: Overnight to Chill

Servings: 1

Ingredients:

- 1/8 cup chia seeds
- 1/2 cup unsweetened nondairy milk
- One tablespoon raw cacao powder
- 1/2 teaspoon vanilla extract
- 1/2 teaspoon pure maple syrup

Directions:

1. Stir together the chia seeds, milk, cacao powder, vanilla, and maple syrup in a large bowl. Divide between 2 (1/2-pint) covered glass jars or containers. Refrigerate overnight.
2. Stir before serving.

Nutrition:

Calories: 213

Fat: 10g

Protein: 9g

Carbohydrates: 20g

Fiber: 15g

Slow Cooker Savory Butternut Squash Oatmeal

Preparation Time: 15 Minutes
Cooking Time: 6 to 8 hours
Servings: 1
Ingredients:

- 1/4 cup steel-cut oats
- 1/2 cups cubed (1/2-inch pieces) peeled butternut squash (freeze any leftovers after preparing a whole squash for future meals)
- 3/4 cups of water
- 1/16 cup unsweetened nondairy milk
- 1/4 tablespoon chia seed
- 1/2 teaspoons yellow (mellow) miso paste
- 3/4 teaspoons ground ginger
- 1/4 tablespoon sesame seed, toasted
- 1/4 tablespoon chopped scallion, green parts only
- Shredded carrot, for serving (optional)

Directions:

1. In a slow cooker, combine the oats, butternut squash, and water.
2. Cover the slow cooker and cook on low for 6 to 8 hours, or until the squash is fork tender. Using a potato

masher or heavy spoon, roughly mash the cooked butternut squash. Stir to combine with the oats.

3. Whisk together the milk, chia seeds, miso paste, and ginger to combine in a large bowl. Stir the mixture into the oats.

4. Top your oatmeal bowl with sesame seeds and scallion for more plant-based fiber, top with shredded carrot (if using).

Nutrition:

Calories: 230

Fat: 5g

Protein: 7g

Carbohydrates: 40g

Fiber: 9g

Carrot Cake Oatmeal

Preparation Time: 10 Minutes

Cooking Time: 15 Minutes

Servings: 1

Ingredients:

- 1/8 cup pecans
- 1/2 cup finely shredded carrot
- 1/4 cup old-fashioned oats
- 5/8 cups unsweetened nondairy milk
- 1/2 tablespoon pure maple syrup
- 1/2 teaspoon ground cinnamon
- 1/2 teaspoon ground ginger
- 1/8 teaspoon ground nutmeg
- One tablespoon chia seed

Directions:

1. Over medium-high heat in a skillet, toast the pecans for 3 to 4 minutes, often stirring, until browned and fragrant (watch closely, as they can burn quickly). Pour the pecans onto a cutting board and coarsely chop them. Set aside.

2. In an 8-quart pot over medium-high heat, combine the carrot, oats, milk, maple syrup, cinnamon, ginger, and nutmeg. When it is already boiling, reduce the heat to medium-low. Cook, uncovered, for 10 minutes, stirring occasionally.

3. Stir in the chopped pecans and chia seeds. Serve immediately.

Nutrition:

Calories: 307

Fat: 17g

Protein: 7g

Carbohydrates: 35g

Fiber: 11g

Spiced Sorghum and Berries

Preparation Time: 5 Minutes

Cooking Time: 1 hour

Servings: 1

Ingredients:

- 1/4 cup whole-grain sorghum
- 1/4 teaspoon ground cinnamon
- 1/4 teaspoon Chinese five-spice powder
- 3/4 cups water
- 1/4 cup unsweetened nondairy milk
- 1/4 teaspoon vanilla extract
- 1/2 tablespoons pure maple syrup
- 1/2 tablespoon chia seed
- 1/8 cup sliced almonds
- 1/2 cups fresh raspberries, divided

Directions:

1. Using a large pot over medium-high heat, stir together the sorghum, cinnamon, five-spice powder, and water. Wait for the water to a boil, cover the bank, and reduce the heat to medium-low. Cook for 1 hour, or until the sorghum is soft and chewy. If the sorghum grains are still hard, add another water cup and cook for 15 minutes more.

2. Using a glass measuring cup, whisk together the milk, vanilla, and maple syrup to blend. Add the mixture to

the sorghum and the chia seeds, almonds, and 1 cup of raspberries. Gently stir to combine.

3. When serving, top with the remaining 1 cup of fresh raspberries.

Nutrition:

Calories: 289

Fat: 8g

Protein: 9g

Carbohydrates: 52g

Fiber: 10g

Dinner

Lemon Garlic Oregano Chicken with Asparagus

Preparation Time: 5 minutes
Cooking Time: 40 minutes
Servings: 4
Ingredients:

- 1 small lemon, juiced (this should be about 2 tablespoons of lemon juice)
- 1 ¾ lb. of bone-in, skinless chicken thighs
- 2 tablespoons of fresh oregano, minced
- 2 cloves of garlic, minced
- 2 lbs. of asparagus, trimmed
- ¼ teaspoon each or less for black pepper and salt

Directions:

1. Preheat the oven to about 3500F.
2. Put the chicken in a medium-sized bowl. Now, add the garlic, oregano, lemon juice, pepper, and salt and toss together to combine.
3. Roast the chicken in the air fryer oven until it reaches an internal temperature of 1650F in about 40 minutes. Once the chicken thighs have been cooked, remove and keep aside to rest.
4. Now, steam the asparagus on a stovetop or in a microwave to the desired doneness.

5. Serve asparagus with the roasted chicken thighs.

Nutrition:

Calories: 350

Fat: 10 g

Carbohydrate: 10 g

Protein: 32 g

Sheet Pan Chicken Fajita Lettuce Wraps

Preparation Time: 15 minutes

Cooking Time: 30 minutes

Servings: 2

Ingredients:

- 1 lb. chicken breast, thinly sliced into strips
- 2 teaspoon of olive oil
- 2 bell peppers, thinly sliced into strips
- 2 teaspoon of fajita seasoning
- 6 leaves from a romaine heart
- Juice of half a lime
- ¼ cup plain of non-fat Greek yogurt

Directions:

1. Preheat your oven to about 4000F

2. Combine all of the ingredients except for lettuce in a large plastic bag that can be resealed. Mix very well to coat vegetables and chicken with oil and seasoning evenly.

3. Spread the contents of the bag evenly on a foil-lined baking sheet. Bake it for about25-30 minutes, until the chicken is thoroughly cooked.

4. Serve on lettuce leaves and topped with Greek yogurt if you like

Nutrition:

Calories: 387

Fat: 6 g

Carbohydrate: 14 g

Protein: 18 g

Savory Cilantro Salmon

Preparation Time: 10 minutes

Cooking Time: 30 minutes

Servings: 4

Ingredients:

- 2 tablespoons of fresh lime or lemon
- 4 cups of fresh cilantro, divided
- 2 tablespoon of hot red pepper sauce
- ½ teaspoon of salt. Divided
- 1 teaspoon of cumin
- 4, 7 oz. of salmon filets
- ½ cup of (4 oz.) water
- 2 cups of sliced red bell pepper
- 2 cups of sliced yellow bell pepper
- 2 cups of sliced green bell pepper
- Cooking spray
- ½ teaspoon of pepper

Directions:

1. Get a blender or food processor and combine half of the cilantro, lime juice or lemon, cumin, hot red pepper sauce, water, and salt; then puree until they become smooth. Transfer the marinade gotten into a large resealable plastic bag.

2. Add salmon to marinade. Seal the bag, squeeze out air that might have been trapped inside, turn to coat salmon. Refrigerate for about 1 hour, turning as often as possible.

3. Now, after marinating, preheat your oven to about 4000F. Arrange the pepper slices in a single layer in a slightly-greased, medium-sized square baking dish. Bake it for 20 minutes, turn the pepper slices once.

4. Drain your salmon and do away with the marinade. Crust the upper part of the salmon with the remaining chopped, fresh cilantro. Place salmon on the top of the pepper slices and bake for about 12-14 minutes until you observe that the fish flakes easily when it is being tested with a fork

5. Enjoy

Nutrition:

Calories: 350

Carbohydrate: 15 g

Protein: 42 g

Fat: 13 g

Salmon Florentine

Preparation Time: 5 minutes

Cooking Time: 30 minutes

Servings: 4

Ingredients:

- 1 ½ cups of chopped cherry tomatoes
- ½ cup of chopped green onions
- 2 garlic cloves, minced
- 1 teaspoon of olive oil
- 1 quantity of 12 oz. package frozen chopped spinach, thawed and patted dry
- ¼ teaspoon of crushed red pepper flakes
- ½ cup of part-skim ricotta cheese
- ¼ teaspoon each for pepper and salt
- 4 quantities of 5 ½ oz. wild salmon fillets
- Cooking spray

Directions:

1. Preheat the oven to 3500F
2. Get a medium skillet to cook onions in oil until they start to soften, which should be in about 2 minutes. You can then add garlic inside the skillet and cook for an extra 1 minute. Add the spinach, red pepper flakes, tomatoes, pepper, and salt. Cook for 2 minutes while stirring. Remove the pan from the heat and let it cool for about 10 minutes. Stir in the ricotta

3. Put a quarter of the spinach mixture on top of each salmon fillet. Place the fillets on a slightly-greased rimmed baking sheet and bake it for 15 minutes or until you are sure that the salmon has been thoroughly cooked.

Nutrition:

Calories: 350

Carbohydrate: 15 g

Protein: 42 g

Fat: 13 g

Tomatillo and Green Chili Pork Stew

Preparation Time: 10 minutes

Cooking Time: 20 minutes

Servings: 4

Ingredients:

- 2 scallions, chopped
- 2 cloves of garlic
- 1 lb. tomatillos, trimmed and chopped
- 8 large romaine or green lettuce leaves, divided
- 2 serrano chilies, seeds, and membranes
- ½ tsp of dried Mexican oregano (or you can use regular oregano)
- 1 ½ lb. of boneless pork loin, to be cut into bite-sized cubes
- ¼ cup of cilantro, chopped
- ¼ tablespoon (each) salt and paper
- 1 jalapeno, seeds and membranes to be removed and thinly sliced
- 1 cup of sliced radishes
- 4 lime wedges

Directions:

1. Combine scallions, garlic, tomatillos, 4 lettuce leaves, serrano chilies, and oregano in a blender. Then puree until smooth

2. Put pork and tomatillo mixture in a medium pot. 1-inch of puree should cover the pork; if not, add water until it covers it. Season with pepper & salt, and cover it simmers. Simmer on heat for approximately 20 minutes.
3. Now, finely shred the remaining lettuce leaves.
4. When the stew is done cooking, garnish with cilantro, radishes, finely shredded lettuce, sliced jalapenos, and lime wedges.

Nutrition:

Calories: 370

Protein: 36g

Carbohydrate: 14g

Fat: 19 g

Meat

Tomato Pork Chops

Preparation Time: 10 minutes

Cooking Time: 6 hours

Servings: 4

Ingredients:

- 4 pork chops, bone-in
- 1 tablespoon garlic, minced
- ½ small onion, chopped
- 6 oz can tomato paste
- 1 bell pepper, chopped
- ¼ teaspoon red pepper flakes
- 1 teaspoon Worcestershire sauce
- 1 tablespoon dried Italian seasoning
- 14.5 oz can tomato, diced
- 2 teaspoon olive oil
- ¼ teaspoon pepper
- 1 teaspoon kosher salt

Directions:

1. Heat oil in a pan over heat.
2. Season pork chops with pepper and salt.
3. Sear pork chops in pan until brown from both the sides.
4. Transfer pork chops into the crock pot.
5. Add remaining ingredients over pork chops.
6. Cover and cook on low heat for 6 hours.

7. Serve and enjoy.

Nutrition:

Calories: 325

Fat: 23.4 g

Carbohydrates: 10 g

Sugar: 6 g

Protein: 20 g

Cholesterol: 70 mg

Greek Pork Chops

Preparation Time: 10 minutes

Cooking Time: 6 minutes

Servings: 8

Ingredients:

- 8 pork chops, boneless
- 4 teaspoon dried oregano
- 2 tablespoon Worcestershire sauce
- 3 tablespoon fresh lemon juice
- ¼ cup olive oil
- 1 teaspoon ground mustard
- 2 teaspoon garlic powder
- 2 teaspoon onion powder
- Pepper
- Salt

Directions:

1. Whisk together oil, garlic powder, onion powder, oregano, Worcestershire sauce, lemon juice, mustard, pepper, and salt.
2. Place pork chops in a dish then pour marinade over pork chops and coat well. Place in refrigerator overnight.
3. Preheat the grill.
4. Place pork chops on the grill and cook for 3-4 minutes on each side.

5. Serve and enjoy.

Nutrition:

Calories: 324

Fat: 26.5 g

Carbohydrates: 2.5 g

Sugar: 1.3 g

Protein: 18 g

Cholesterol: 69 mg

Pork Cacciatore

Preparation Time: 10 minutes

Cooking Time: 6 hours

Servings: 6

Ingredients:

- 1 ½ lbs pork chops
- 1 teaspoon dried oregano
- 1 cup beef broth
- 3 tablespoon tomato paste
- 14 oz can tomato, diced
- 2 cups mushrooms, sliced
- 1 small onion, diced
- 1 garlic clove, minced
- 2 tablespoon olive oil
- ¼ teaspoon pepper
- ½ teaspoon salt

Directions:

1. Heat oil in a pan over medium heat.
2. Add pork chops in pan and cook until brown on both the sides.
3. Transfer pork chops into the crock pot.
4. Pour remaining ingredients over the pork chops.
5. Cover and cook on low heat for 6 hours.
6. Serve and enjoy.

Nutrition:

Calories: 440

Fat: 33 g

Carbohydrates: 6 g

Sugar: 3 g

Protein: 28 g

Cholesterol: 97 mg

Pork with Tomato & Olives

Preparation Time: 10 minutes

Cooking Time: 30 minutes

Servings: 6

Ingredients:

6 pork chops, boneless and cut into thick slices

1/8 teaspoon ground cinnamon

1/2 cup olives, pitted and sliced

8 oz can tomato, crushed

1/4 cup beef broth

2 garlic cloves, chopped

1 large onion, sliced

1 tablespoon olive oil

Directions:

Heat olive oil in a pan over medium heat.

Place pork chops in a pan and cook until lightly brown and set aside.

Cook onion and garlic in the same pan over medium heat, until onion is softened.

Add broth and bring to boil over high heat.

Return pork to pan and stir in crushed tomatoes and remaining ingredients.

Cover and simmer for 20 minutes.

Serve and enjoy.

Nutrition:

Calories: 321

Fat: 23 g

Carbohydrates: 7 g

Sugar: 1 g

Protein: 19 g

Cholesterol: 70 mg

Seafood

Salmon Burgers

Preparation Time: 10 minutes

Cooking Time: 15 minutes

Serving: 4

Ingredients:

- 1 lb. salmon fillets
- 1 onion
- ¼ dill fronds
- 1 tablespoon honey
- 1 tablespoon horseradish
- 1 tablespoon mustard
- 1 tablespoon olive oil
- 2 toasted split rolls
- 1 avocado

Directions:

1. Place salmon fillets in a blender and blend until smooth, transfer to a bowl, add onion, dill, honey, horseradish and mix well
2. Season with salt and pepper and form 4 patties
3. In a bowl combine mustard, honey, mayonnaise and dill
4. In a skillet heat oil add salmon patties and cook for 2-3 minutes per side
5. When ready remove from heat
6. Divided lettuce and onion between the buns

7. Place salmon patty on top and spoon mustard mixture and avocado slices

8. Serve when ready

Nutrition:

Calories: 189

Total Carbohydrate: 6 g

Cholesterol: 3 mg

Total Fat: 7 g

Fiber: 4 g

Protein: 12 g

Sodium: 293 mg

Seared Scallops

Preparation Time: 15 minutes

Cooking Time: 20 minutes

Serving: 4

Ingredients:

- 1 lb. sea scallops
- 1 tablespoon canola oil

Directions:

1. Season scallops and refrigerate for a couple of minutes
2. In a skillet heat oil, add scallops and cook for 1-2 minutes per side
3. When ready remove from heat and serve

Nutrition:

Calories: 283

Total Carbohydrate: 10 g

Cholesterol: 3 mg

Total Fat: 8 g

Fiber: 2 g

Protein: 9 g

Sodium: 271 mg

Black COD

Preparation Time: 15 minutes

Cooking Time: 20 minutes

Serving: 4

Ingredients:

- ¼ cup miso paste
- ¼ cup sake
- 1 tablespoon mirin
- 1 teaspoon soy sauce
- 1 tablespoon olive oil
- 4 black cod filets

Directions:

1. In a bowl combine miso, soy sauce, oil and sake
2. Rub mixture over cod fillets and let it marinade for 20-30 minutes
3. Adjust broiler and broil cod filets for 10-12 minutes
4. When fish is cook remove and serve

Nutrition:

Calories: 231

Total Carbohydrate: 2 g

Cholesterol: 13 mg

Total Fat: 15 g

Fiber: 2 g

Protein: 8 g

Sodium: 298 mg

Miso-Glazed Salmon

Preparation Time: 10 minutes

Cooking Time: 40 minutes

Serving: 4

Ingredients:

- ¼ cup red miso
- ¼ cup sake
- 1 tablespoon soy sauce
- 1 tablespoon vegetable oil
- 4 salmon fillets

Directions:

1. In a bowl combine sake, oil, soy sauce and miso
2. Rub mixture over salmon fillets and marinade for 20-30 minutes
3. Preheat a broiler
4. Broil salmon for 5-10 minutes
5. When ready remove and serve

Nutrition:

Calories: 198

Total Carbohydrate: 5 g

Cholesterol: 12 mg

Total Fat: 10 g

Fiber: 2 g

Protein: 6 g

Sodium: 257 mg

Vegetables

Fried Avocado

Preparation time: 15 minutes

Cooking time: 10 minutes

Servings: 2

Ingredients:

- 2 avocados cut into wedges 25 mm thick
- 50g Pan crumbs bread
- 2g garlic powder
- 2g onion powder
- 1g smoked paprika
- 1g cayenne pepper
- Salt and pepper to taste
- 60g all-purpose flour
- 2 eggs, beaten
- Nonstick Spray Oil
- Tomato sauce or ranch sauce, to serve

Directions:

1. Cut the avocados into 25 mm thick pieces.
2. Combine the crumbs, garlic powder, onion powder, smoked paprika, cayenne pepper and salt in a bowl.
3. Separate each wedge of avocado in the flour, then dip the beaten eggs and stir in the breadcrumb mixture.
4. Preheat the air fryer.

5. Place the avocados in the preheated air fryer baskets, spray with oil spray and cook at 205°C for 10 minutes. Turn the fried avocado halfway through cooking and sprinkle with cooking oil.
6. Serve with tomato sauce or ranch sauce.

Nutrition:

Calories: 123

Carbs: 2 g

Fat: 11 g

Protein: 4 g

Fiber: 0 g

Vegetables in air Fryer

Preparation time: 20 minutes

Cooking time: 30 minutes

Servings: 2

Ingredients:

- 2 potatoes
- 1 zucchini
- 1 onion
- 1 red pepper
- 1 green pepper

Directions:

1. Cut the potatoes into slices.
2. Cut the onion into rings.
3. Cut the zucchini slices
4. Cut the peppers into strips.
5. Put all the ingredients in the bowl and add a little salt, ground pepper and some extra virgin olive oil.
6. Mix well.
7. Pass to the basket of the air fryer.
8. Select 160oC, 30 minutes.
9. Check that the vegetables are to your liking.

Nutrition:

Calories: 135

Carbs: 2 g

Fat: 11 g

Protein: 4 g

Fiber: 05g

Crispy Rye Bread Snacks with Guacamole and Anchovies

Preparation time: 10 minutes

Cooking time: 10 minutes

Servings: 4

Ingredients:

- 4 slices of rye bread
- Guacamole
- Anchovies in oil

Directions:

1. Cut each slice of bread into 3 strips of bread.
2. Place in the basket of the air fryer, without piling up, and we go in batches giving it the touch you want to give it. You can select 1800C, 10 minutes.
3. When you have all the crusty rye bread strips, put a layer of guacamole on top, whether homemade or commercial.
4. In each bread, place 2 anchovies on the guacamole.

Nutrition:

Calories: 180

Carbs: 4 g

Fat: 11 g

Protein: 4 g

Fiber: 09 g

Soup and Stew

Cream of Thyme Tomato Soup

Preparation Time: 5 minutes

Cooking Time: 20 minutes

Servings: 6

Ingredients:

- 2 tbsp ghee
- 2 large red onions, diced
- 1/2 cup raw cashew nuts, diced
- 2 (28 oz.) cans tomatoes
- 1 tsp. fresh thyme leaves + extra to garnish
- 1 1/2 cups water
- Salt and black pepper to taste

Directions:

1. Melt ghee in a pot over medium heat and sauté the onions for 4 minutes until softened.
2. Stir in the tomatoes, thyme, water, cashews, and season with salt and black pepper.
3. Cover and bring to simmer for 10 minutes until thoroughly cooked.
4. Open, turn the heat off, and puree the ingredients with an immersion blender.
5. Adjust to taste and stir in the heavy cream.
6. Spoon into soup bowls and serve.

Nutrition:

Calories: 310 Cal

Fats: 27 g

Carbohydrates: 3g

Protein: 11g

Mushroom & Jalapeño Stew

Preparation Time: 20 minutes

Cooking Time: 50 minutes

Servings: 4

Ingredients:

- 2 tsp. olive oil
- 1 cup leeks, chopped
- 1 garlic clove, minced
- 1/2 cup celery stalks, chopped
- 1/2 cup carrots, chopped
- 1 green bell pepper, chopped
- 1 jalapeño pepper, chopped
- 2 1/2 cups mushrooms, sliced
- 1 1/2 cups vegetable stock
- 2 tomatoes, chopped
- 2 thyme sprigs, chopped
- 1 rosemary sprig, chopped
- 2 bay leaves
- 1/2 tsp. salt
- 1/4 tsp. ground black pepper
- 2 tbsp vinegar

Directions:

1. Set a pot over medium heat and warm oil.

2. Add in garlic and leeks and sauté until soft and translucent.
3. Add in the black pepper, celery, mushrooms, and carrots.
4. Cook as you stir for 12 minutes; stir in a splash of vegetable stock to ensure there is no sticking.
5. Stir in the rest of the ingredients.
6. Set heat to medium; allow to simmer for 25 to 35 minutes or until cooked through.
7. Divide into individual bowls and serve warm.

Nutrition:

Calories: 65 Cal

Fats: 2.7 g

Carbohydrates: 9 g

Protein: 2.7 g

Easy Cauliflower Soup

Preparation Time: 5 minutes

Cooking Time: 15 minutes

Servings: 4

Ingredients:

- 2 tbsp olive oil
- 2 onions, finely chopped
- 1 tsp. garlic, minced
- 1 pound cauliflower, cut into florets
- 1 cup kale, chopped
- 4 cups vegetable broth
- 1/2 cup almond milk
- 1/2 tsp. salt
- 1/2 tsp. red pepper flakes
- 1 tbsp fresh chopped parsley

Directions:

1. Set a pot over medium heat and warm the oil.
2. Add garlic and onions and sauté until browned and softened.
3. Place in vegetable broth, kale, and cauliflower; cook for 10 minutes until the mixture boils.
4. Stir in the pepper flakes, salt, and almond milk; reduce the heat and simmer the soup for 5 minutes.

5. Transfer the soup to an immersion blender and blend to achieve the desired consistency; top with parsley and serve immediately.

Nutrition:

Calories: 172 Cal

Fats: 10.3 g

Carbohydrates: 11.8g

Protein: 8.1 g

Main

Cheesy Cauliflower Fritters

Preparation Time: 10 Minutes

Cooking Time: 7 Minutes

Servings: 1

Ingredients:

- 1/2 C. chopped parsley
- 1 C. Italian breadcrumbs
- 1/3 C. shredded mozzarella cheese
- 1/3 C. shredded sharp cheddar cheese
- One egg
- Two minced garlic cloves
- Three chopped scallions
- One head of cauliflower

Directions:

1. Preparing the Ingredients. Cut the cauliflower up into florets. Wash well and pat dry. Place into a food processor and pulse 20-30 seconds till it looks like rice.
2. Place the cauliflower rice in a bowl and mix with pepper, salt, egg, cheeses, breadcrumbs, garlic, and scallions.
3. With hands, form 15 patties of the mixture then add more breadcrumbs if needed.
4. Air Frying. With olive oil, spritz patties, and put the fitters into your Instant Crisp Air Fryer. Pile it in a single layer. Lock the air fryer lid. Set temperature to

390°F, and set time to 7 minutes, flipping after 7 minutes.

Nutrition:

Calories: 209

Fat: 17g

Protein: 6g

Sugar: 0.5

Zucchini Parmesan Chips

Preparation Time: 10 Minutes

Cooking Time: 8 Minutes

Servings: 1

Ingredients:

- 1/2 tsp. paprika
- 1/2 C. grated parmesan cheese
- 1/2 C. Italian breadcrumbs
- One lightly beaten egg
- Two thinly sliced zucchinis

Directions:

1. Preparing the Ingredients. Use a very sharp knife or mandolin slicer to slice zucchini as thinly as you can. Pat off extra moisture.
2. Beat egg with a pinch of pepper and salt and a bit of water.
3. Combine paprika, cheese, and breadcrumbs in a bowl.
4. Dip slices of zucchini into the egg mixture and then into breadcrumb mixture. Press gently to coat.
5. Air Frying. With olive oil cooking spray, mist encrusted zucchini slices. Put into your Instant Crisp Air Fryer in a single layer. Latch the air fryer lid. Set temperature to 350°F and set time to 8 minutes.
6. Sprinkle with salt and serve with salsa.

Nutrition:

Calories: 211

Fat: 16g

Protein: 8g

Sugar: 0g

Jalapeno Cheese Balls

Preparation Time: 10 Minutes

Cooking Time: 8 Minutes

Servings: 1

Ingredients:

- 1-ounce cream cheese
- 1/6 cup shredded mozzarella cheese
- 1/6 cup shredded Cheddar cheese
- 1/2 jalapeños, finely chopped
- 1/2 cup breadcrumbs
- Two eggs
- 1/2 cup all-purpose flour
- Salt
- Pepper
- Cooking oil

Directions:

1. Preparing the Ingredients. Combine the cream cheese, mozzarella, Cheddar, and jalapeños in a medium bowl. Mix well.
2. Form the cheese mixture into balls about an inch thick. You may also use a small ice cream scoop. It works well.
3. Arrange the cheese balls on a sheet pan and place in the freezer for 15 minutes. It will help the cheese balls maintain their shape while frying.

4. Spray the Instant Crisp Air Fryer basket with cooking oil. Place the breadcrumbs in a small bowl. In another small bowl, beat the eggs. In the third small bowl, combine the flour with salt and pepper to taste, and mix well. Remove the cheese balls from the freezer. Plunge the cheese balls in the flour, then the eggs, and then the breadcrumbs.

5. Air Frying. Place the cheese balls in the Instant Crisp Air Fryer. Spray with cooking oil. Lock the air fryer lid— Cook for 8 minutes.

6. Open the Instant Crisp Air Fryer and flip the cheese balls. I recommend flipping them instead of shaking, so the balls maintain their form. Cook an additional 4 minutes. Cool before serving.

Nutrition:

Calories: 96

Fat: 6g

Protein: 4g

Sugar: 0g

Crispy Roasted Broccoli

Preparation Time: 10 Minutes

Cooking Time: 8 Minutes

Servings: 1

Ingredients:

- 1/4 tsp. Masala
- 1/2 tsp. red chili powder
- 1/2 tsp. salt
- 1/4 tsp. turmeric powder
- 1 tbsp. chickpea flour
- 1 tbsp. yogurt
- 1/2-pound broccoli

Directions:

1. Preparing the Ingredients. Cut broccoli up into florets. Immerse in a bowl of water with two teaspoons of salt for at least half an hour to remove impurities.

2. Take out broccoli florets from water and let drain. Wipe down thoroughly.

3. Mix all other ingredients to create a marinade.

4. Toss broccoli florets in the marinade. Cover and chill 15-30 minutes.

5. Air Frying. Preheat the Instant Crisp Air Fryer to 390 degrees. Place marinated broccoli florets into the fryer, lock the air fryer lid, set the temperature to 350°F, and

set time to 10 minutes. Florets will be crispy when done.

Nutrition:

Calories: 96

Fat: 1.3g

Protein: 7g

Sugar: 4.5g

Sides

Coconut Fat Bombs

Preparation Time: 2 minutes

Cooking Time: 10 minutes

Servings: 4

Ingredients:

- 2/3 cup coconut oil, melted
- 1 (14 oz.) can coconut milk
- 18 drops stevia liquid
- 1 cup unsweetened coconut flakes

Directions:

1. Mix the coconut oil with the milk and stevia to combine.
2. Stir in the coconut flakes until well distributed.
3. Pour into silicone muffin molds and freeze for 1 hour to harden.

Nutrition:

Calories: 214 Cal

Fat: 19 g

Carbohydrates: 2 g

Protein: 4 g

Tomato Cucumber Avocado Salad

Preparation Time: 5 minutes

Cooking Time: 15 minutes

Servings: 4

Ingredients:

- 12 oz. cherry tomatoes, cut in half
- 5 small cucumbers, chopped
- 3 small avocados, chopped
- 1/2 tsp. ground black pepper
- 2 tbsp olive oil
- 2 tbsp fresh lemon juice
- 1/4 cup fresh cilantro, chopped
- 1 tsp. sea salt

Directions:

1. Add cherry tomatoes, cucumbers, avocados, and cilantro into the large mixing bowl and mix well.
2. Mix olive oil, lemon juice, black pepper, and salt and pour over salad.
3. Toss well and serve immediately.

Nutrition:

Calories: 442 Cal

Fat: 37.1 g

Carbohydrates: 30.3 g

Sugar: 9.4 g

Protein: 6.2 g

Cholesterol: 0 mg

Easy One-Pot Vegan Marinara

Preparation Time: 5 minutes

Cooking Time: 15 minutes

Servings: 2

Ingredients:

- 1 cup water
- 1 cup tomato paste
- 2 tablespoons maple syrup
- 1 teaspoon dried oregano
- 1 teaspoon dried thyme
- 1 teaspoon garlic powder
- 1 teaspoon onion powder
- 1/2 teaspoon dried basil
- 1/4 teaspoon red pepper flakes

Directions:

1. In a medium saucepan, bring the water to a rolling boil over high heat.
2. Reduce the heat to low, and whisk in the tomato paste, maple syrup, oregano, thyme, garlic powder, onion powder, basil, and red pepper flakes.
3. Cover and simmer for 10 minutes, stirring occasionally. Serve warm.

Nutrition:

Fat: 0g

Carbohydrates: 17 g

Fiber: 3 g

Protein: 3 g

Snacks

Cinnamon Bites

Preparation Time: 20 minutes

Cooking Time: 95 minutes

Servings: 6

Ingredients:

- 1/8 Teaspoon Nutmeg
- 1 Teaspoon Vanilla Extract
- ¼ Teaspoon Cinnamon
- 4 Tablespoons Coconut Oil
- ½ Cup Butter, Grass Fed
- 8 Ounces Cream Cheese
- Stevia to Taste

Directions:

1. Soften your coconut oil and butter, mixing in your cream cheese.
2. Add all of your remaining ingredients, and mix well.
3. Pour into molds, and freeze until set.

Nutrition:

Calories: 178

Protein: 1

Fat: 19

Sweet Chai Bites

Preparation Time: 20 minutes

Cooking Time: 45 minutes

Servings: 6

Ingredients:

- 1 Cup Cream Cheese
- 1 Cup Coconut Oil
- 2 Ounces Butter, Grass Fed
- 2 Teaspoons Ginger
- 2 Teaspoons Cardamom
- 1 Teaspoon Nutmeg
- 1 Teaspoon Cloves
- 1 Teaspoon Vanilla Extract, Pure
- 1 Teaspoon Darjeeling Black Tea
- Stevia to Taste

Directions:

1. Melt your coconut oil and butter before adding in your black tea. Allow it to set for one to two minutes.
2. Add in your cream cheese, removing your mixture from heat.
3. Add in all of your spices, and stir to combine.
4. Pour into molds, and freeze before serving.

Nutrition:

Calories: 178

Protein: 1

Fat: 19

Easy Vanilla Bombs

Preparation Time: 20 minutes

Cooking Time: 45 minutes

Servings: 14

Ingredients:

- 1 Cup Macadamia Nuts, Unsalted
- ¼ Cup Coconut Oil / ¼ Cup Butter
- 2 Teaspoons Vanilla Extract, Sugar Free
- 20 Drops Liquid Stevia
- 2 Tablespoons Erythritol, Powdered

Directions:

1. Pulse your macadamia nuts in a blender, and then combine all of your ingredients together. Mix well.
2. Get out mini muffin tins with a tablespoon and a half of the mixture.
3. Refrigerate it for a half hour before serving.

Nutrition:

Calories:125

Fat: 5

Carbohydrates: 5

Marinated Eggs.

Preparation Time: 2 hours and 10 minutes
Cooking Time: 7 minutes
Servings: 4
Ingredients:

- 6 eggs
- 1 and ¼ cups water
- ¼ cup unsweetened rice vinegar 2 tablespoons coconut aminos
- Salt and black pepper to the taste 2 garlic cloves, minced
- 1 teaspoon stevia 4 ounces cream cheese
- 1 tablespoon chives, chopped

Directions:

1. Put the eggs in a pot, add water to cover, bring to a boil over medium heat, cover and cook for 7 minutes.
2. Rinse eggs with cold water and leave them aside to cool down.
3. In a bowl, mix 1 cup water with coconut aminos, vinegar, stevia and garlic and whisk well.
4. Put the eggs in this mix, cover with a kitchen towel and leave them aside for 2 hours rotating from time to time.
5. Peel eggs, cut in halves and put egg yolks in a bowl.
6. Add ¼ cup water, cream cheese, salt, pepper and chives and stir well.

7. Stuff egg whites with this mix and serve them.

8. Enjoy!

Nutrition:

Calories: 289 kcal

Protein: 15.86 g

Fat: 22.62 g

Carbohydrates: 4.52 g

Sodium: 288 mg

Dessert

Braised Apples

Preparation Time: 5 minutes

Cooking Time: 12 minutes

Servings: 2

Ingredients:

- 2 cored apples
- ½ cup of water
- ½ cup red wine
- 3 tbsp. sugar
- ½ tsp. ground cinnamon

Directions:

1. In the bottom of Instant Pot, add the water and place apples.
2. Pour wine on top and sprinkle with sugar and cinnamon.
3. Close the lid carefully and cook for 10 minutes at HIGH PRESSURE.
4. When done, do a quick pressure release.
5. Transfer the apples onto serving plates and top with cooking liquid.
6. Serve immediately.

Nutrition

Calories: 245

Fat: 0.5 g

Carbs: 53 g

Protein: 1 g

Wine Figs

Preparation Time: 5 minutes

Cooking Time: 3 minutes

Servings: 2

Ingredients:

- ½ cup pine nuts
- 1 cup red wine
- 1 lb. figs
- Sugar, as needed

Directions:

1. Slowly pour the wine and sugar into the Instant Pot.
2. Arrange the trivet inside it; place the figs over it. Close the lid and lock. Ensure that you have sealed the valve to avoid leakage.
3. Press MANUAL mode and set timer to 3 minutes.
4. After the timer reads zero, press CANCEL and quick-release pressure.
5. Carefully remove the lid.
6. Divide figs into bowls, and drizzle wine from the pot over them.
7. Top with pine nuts and enjoy.

Nutrition

Calories: 95

Fat: 3 g

Carbs: 5 g

Protein: 2 g

Lemon Curd

Preparation Time: 10 minutes

Cooking Time: 10 minutes

Servings: 2

Ingredients:

- 4 tbsp. butter
- 1 cup sugar
- 2/3 cup lemon juice
- 3 eggs
- 2 tsp. lemon zest
- 1 ½ cups of water

Directions:

1. Whisk the butter and sugar thoroughly until smooth.
2. Add 2 whole eggs and incorporate just the yolk of the other egg.
3. Add the lemon juice.
4. Transfer the mixture into the two jars and tightly seal the tops
5. Pour 1 ½ cups of water into the bottom of the Instant Pot and place in steaming rack. Put the jars on the rack and cook on HIGH PRESSURE for 10 minutes.
6. Natural-release the pressure for 10 minutes before quick releasing the rest.
7. Stir in the zest and put the lids back on the jars.

Nutrition

Calories: 45

Fat: 1 g

Carbs: 8 g

Protein: 1 g

Rhubarb Dessert

Preparation Time: 4 minutes

Cooking Time: 5 minutes

Servings: 2

Ingredients:

- 3 cups rhubarb, chopped
- 1 tbsp. ghee, melted
- 1/3 cup water
- 1 tbsp. stevia
- 1 tsp. vanilla extract

Directions:

1. Put all the listed Ingredients: in your Instant Pot, cover, and cook on HIGH for 5 minutes.
2. Divide into small bowls and serve cold.
3. Enjoy!

Nutrition

Calories: 83

Fat: 2 g

Carbs: 2 g

Protein: 2 g

Raspberry Compote

Preparation Time: 11 minutes

Cooking Time: 30 minutes

Servings: 2

Ingredients:

- 1 cup raspberries
- ½ cup Swerve
- 1 tsp freshly grated lemon zest
- 1 tsp vanilla extract
- 2 cups water

Directions:

1. Press the SAUTÉ button on your Instant Pot, then add all the listed ingredients
2. Stir well and pour in 1 cup of water.
3. Cook for 5 minutes, continually stirring, then pour in 1 more cup of water and press the CANCEL button.
4. Secure the lid properly, press the MANUAL button, and set the timer to 15 minutes on LOW pressure.
5. When the timer buzzes, press the CANCEL button and release the pressure naturally for 10minutes.
6. Move the pressure handle to the "venting" position to release any remaining pressure and open the lid.
7. Let it cool before serving.

Nutrition:

Calories: 48

Fat: 0.5 g

Carbs: 5 g

Protein: 1 g

Poached Pears

Preparation Time: 8 minutes

Cooking Time: 10 minutes

Servings: 2

Ingredients:

- 1 tbsp. lime juice
- 2 tsp. lime zest
- 1 cinnamon stick
- 2 whole pears, peeled
- 1 cup of water
- Fresh mint leaves for garnish

Directions:

1. Add all Ingredients: except for the mint leaves to the Instant Pot.
2. Seal the Instant Pot and choose the MANUAL button.
3. Cook on HIGH for 10 minutes.
4. Perform a natural pressure release.
5. Remove the pears from the pot.
6. Serve in bowls and garnish with mint on top.

Nutrition

Calories: 59

Fat: 0.1 g

Carbs: 14 g

Protein: 0.3 g

Apple Crisp

Preparation Time: 10 minutes

Cooking Time: 13 minutes

Servings: 2

Ingredients:

- 2 apples, sliced into chunks
- 1 tsp. cinnamon
- ¼ cup rolled oats
- 1/4 cup brown sugar
- ½ cup of water

Directions :

1. Put all the listed Ingredients: in the pot and mix well.
2. Seal the pot, choose MANUAL mode, and cook at HIGH pressure for 8 minutes.
3. Release the pressure naturally and let sit for 5 minutes or until the sauce has thickened.
4. Serve and enjoy.

Nutrition

Calories: 218

Fat: 5 mg

Carbs: 54 g

Chocolate Bars

Preparation Time: 10 minutes

Cooking Time: 20 minutes

Servings: 16

Ingredients:

- 15 oz cream cheese, softened
- 15 oz unsweetened dark chocolate
- 1 tsp vanilla
- 10 drops liquid stevia

Directions:

1. Grease 8-inch square dish and set aside.
2. In a saucepan dissolve chocolate over low heat.
3. Add stevia and vanilla and stir well.
4. Remove pan from heat and set aside.
5. Add cream cheese into the blender and blend until smooth.
6. Add melted chocolate mixture into the cream cheese and blend until just combined.
7. Transfer mixture into the prepared dish and spread evenly and place in the refrigerator until firm.
8. Slice and serve.

Nutrition:

Calories: 230

Fat: 24 g

Carbs: 7.5 g

Sugar: 0.1 g

Protein: 6 g

Cholesterol: 29 mg

Blueberry Muffins

Preparation Time: 15 minutes

Cooking Time: 35 minutes

Servings: 12

Ingredients:

- 2 eggs
- 1/2 cup fresh blueberries
- 1 cup heavy cream
- 2 cups almond flour
- 1/4 tsp lemon zest
- 1/2 tsp lemon extract
- 1 tsp baking powder
- 5 drops stevia
- 1/4 cup butter, melted

Directions:

1. heat the cooker to 350 F. Line muffin tin with cupcake liners and set aside.
2. Add eggs into the bowl and whisk until mix.
3. Add remaining ingredients and mix to combine.
4. Pour mixture into the prepared muffin tin and bake for 25 minutes.
5. Serve and enjoy.

Nutrition:

Calories: 190

Fat: 17 g

Carbs: 5 g

Sugar: 1 g

Protein: 5 g

Cholesterol: 55 mg

CPSIA information can be obtained
at www.ICGtesting.com
Printed in the USA
BVHW090118240521
607867BV00003B/896